ROBERT MAASS

When Summer Comes

Henry Holt and Company · New York

This book is dedicated
to a summer in North Branch.

Henry Holt and Company, LLC, *Publishers since 1866*
115 West 18th Street, New York, New York 10011

Henry Holt is a registered trademark of Henry Holt and Company, LLC

Distributed in Canada by H. B. Fenn and Company Ltd.

Library of Congress Cataloging-in-Publication Data
Maass, Robert.
When summer comes / by Robert Maass.
Summary: Text and photographs depict the typical activities of summer.
1. Summer—Juvenile literature. [1. Summer.] I. Title.
QB637.6.M3   1993   508—dc20   92-26955

ISBN 0-8050-4706-9
3 5 7 9 10 8 6 4 2

First published in hardcover in 1993 by Henry Holt and Company
First Owlet paperback edition—1996
Printed in Hong Kong

When school lets out

and sun pours down…

that's when summer comes.

Early in summer the first fruits are ripe for eating.

Fresh-picked vegetables appear at roadside stands.

Fifers march
and fireworks flare

when the corn's knee-high
on the Fourth of July.

Bugs wake up when summer comes.
Caterpillars crawl, butterflies alight,
Water-skippers cast shadows
in ponds.

Fat bees hover.

Water's best in summertime. Cool and clear,
it gushes from a sprinkler or tosses breezes at the beach

or swirls in a rushing stream.

It's also the place to catch fish.

Summer is a time
for street fairs
sandwiched between
city buildings.
The hot summer night is
filled with brassy music,
lights, and magic.

Country fairs under
bright summer skies
mean food and games and fun,
a place to show prize animals
(or take a break in the shade).

Baseball makes
summer dreams
come true.

When summer comes, a hot dog from the grill

or a slice of
juicy watermelon
is better than a fancy meal.

There's money
to be made,

and money to be spent.

Summer is a time for new experiences

and old-fashioned pleasures.

When the last stalks tower and the flowers are full-blown,

it's time to gather summer's late harvest.

There's one more swing to try, one more ride to take,

and one more day at the beach. Then, much too soon,
a cool breeze blows, and summer slips away.

It's hard to say good-bye to summer.